# Oh no, I've lost my job;
# What am I going to do?

**The Survivors Guide to Unemployment**

**Practical advice on what to do if you lose your job from someone who knows what it's like – it happened to me too.**

**DAVID JONES**

74174

137

# Oh no; I've lost my job. What am I going to do?

## David Jones

**Dedicated to my children Edward, Victoria and Rebecca; and to Pauline**

### Acknowledgements:

This book would not be possible without the help and assistance of so many people.

I would like to acknowledge the help given by:

Gemini International Ltd – for printing and publishing the book
TQ Paper Ltd – for supplying the paper on which the book is printed
Davy McDonald – for the cover design
Rachel Early – who designed the website www.joblessandproud.com
Gordon Murray – who built the website www.joblessandproud.com
Maryrose Lyons – who co-ordinated the www.joblessandproud.com project
Alex Gibson – who organised the podcasts
David Duignan – who did the photography
Andy Pritchard – who designed and built the website www.thejobseekersunion.com

**Published by Gemini International Ltd**
Printed in Ireland by Gemini International Ltd

Copyright © 2009 David Jones

The moral right of the author has been asserted

A CIP catalogue record for this book is available from the British Library

ISBN 978-0-9562303-0-0

**Join the Job Seekers Union and help unemployed people help themselves.
Register now at www.thejobseekersunion.com**

# Oh no, I've lost my job; what am I going to do now?

## Copyright David Jones 2009

The right of David Jones to be identified as author of this work has been asserted by him in accordance with the copyright, design and patents acts pertaining.

All rights reserved. No reproduction, copy or transmission of this work may be made without written permission from the author.

No paragraph of this work may be reproduced, copied or transmitted save with written permission of the author or in accordance with the provisions of the copyright acts pertaining.

This work is made available subject to the condition that it shall not, by way of trade or otherwise, be lent, sold, hired out or otherwise circulated without the author's prior consent.

Any person who does any unauthorized act in relation to this work may be liable to criminal prosecution and civil claim for damages.

"We're really sorry; sales are down, the company's losing money, the recession's bad, we're merging, being taken over, closing down; whatever it is – we're going to have to let you go!"

You feel numb, you're in shock; you're angry, frightened, embarrassed, ashamed. You don't know what to say. It's not fair; I don't deserve this. Why me?

You think of the kids, the wife; the mortgage. Oh my god, what am I going to do?

They thank you for all your hard work, try to reassure you, tell you it'll be all right; something's bound to come up. They shake your hand, wish you luck.

You say goodbye; and suddenly you're all alone.

You're unemployed; you're on your own. It's your problem. What are you going to do?

Oh no, I've lost my job; what am I going to do now?

## Read this little book; it will help:
- How will you cope with losing your job?
- What are the financial implications?
- What are your entitlements?
  - Notice period
  - Redundancy payments
  - Unemployment & other benefits
- How do you go about getting another job?
- How do you prepare a CV?
- What if you're unemployed for a long term?
- Where can you go to get help?

# Join the Job Seekers Union at www.thejobseekersunion.com

Oh no, I've lost my job; what am I going to do now?

# -CONTENTS-

Oh no, I've lost my job; what am I going to do now?

# Real life experiences turn theory into practice

Oh no, I've lost my job; what am I going to do now?

# MY STORY – It happened to me too!

I didn't see it coming. The first inclination I got was Tuesday lunchtime. I got a phone call to say the owners of the company wanted to see me. I knew things weren't great with the business. They hadn't been for sometime; but I thought we had a plan to deal with that.

"We've decided to close the company down. You've been doing a good job, but sales are declining. We're letting everybody go. You're entitled to a week's notice. We have a cheque here for you. You can go home now; you needn't come in tomorrow. We'll give you a good reference."

That was it; that was my welcome to the world of unemployment. No announcement in the newspapers or on the TV that my job was about to go. Not a gentle little nudge, no time to get used to the idea; no farewell party, no real chance to say good bye to friends and colleagues. Talk about a short sharp shock!

I'm 57 by the way; if I was a policeman I'd be retired with a nice government pension. But I'm not a retired policeman and I don't have a pension. I'm a separated, hard-working middle manager with kids in college, an overdraft, a couple of maxed out credit cards and an income tax bill that needs to be settled. I'd been with the Company 14 months. I'd worked really hard, often staying late and regularly taking work home. I didn't qualify for redundancy or compensation for loss of office or anything like that. All I got was a week's pay in lieu of notice.

I've never been unemployed before. This is a whole new experience for me. It's not one that I would have wanted; but it is one that I am going to have to learn to live with.

I decided to write this little book for a couple of reasons:

- I really do hope it will help people like me who lose their jobs and don't know what to do
- I've always wanted to be a writer

I also believe that it doesn't really matter what happens in life; it is your reaction to it that really counts. This is my reaction to losing my job; if it helps others who find themselves in my situation, it would have been worth it.

*'Everything happens for a reason!'*

**God, grant me:**
**The serenity to accept the things I**
**cannot change,**
**The courage to change the things I**
**can;**
**And the wisdom to know the**
**difference!**

Oh no, I've lost my job; what am I going to do now?

# FIRST REACTIONS
## To being told you've lost your job

Losing your job is one of the most harrowing things that can happen to anyone. It ranks alongside bereavement and divorce as one of the major traumas that can have a negative impact on your life. The recession that's gripping the Western world right now, and the resultant uncertainty about future employment, makes it doubly traumatic.

Don't be surprised if your first reaction to hearing the news, that you've lost your job, is numbness. The body naturally shuts down temporarily to protect itself at times of stress. Later, after the news has sunk in, you may suffer from delayed shock. You might feel nauseous, shaky or light-headed; you might even suffer a panic attack. These are all normal reactions to the bad news you've just received. Don't be alarmed if you feel overwhelmed; time, and positive thinking, will help settle things down.

You might also feel angry, confused, frightened, embarrassed or even ashamed. The natural reaction is to wonder why? "Why is this happening to me? What have I done wrong? Could I, or should I, have done things differently? Where is this recession going to end?"

The truthful answer is God alone knows what is going on. Recessions are cyclical things; they come and go. This one is probably overdue. Unfortunately it's probably also going to be a bad one that might last for several years.

As to why you? Well, why not you?

Everyone else is suffering from the economic catastrophe that's enveloping the world. It's the times we live in; wrong place, wrong time. It's as simple as that.

Could you, should you, have done things differently? Do me a favour. You didn't cause the recession. It's not your fault you're losing your job. It's Bush and the bankers, the property bubble of the Celtic Tiger, and the credit crunch that have got us all into this mess.

Don't blame yourself, don't blame me; don't blame anyone in particular. No one saw it coming; and no one seems to know what to do to stop it now it's started. So don't waste your time on self analysis and soul searching. Unless, that is, you happen to be George W Bush, or Brian Cowan, or Gordon Brown. (Oh my God, if you're one of those three and you're reading this little book, then we're in even bigger trouble than I thought we were!)

Honestly my friend, it's not fault you've lost your job; you're not to blame. There's nothing different you could have done. Not unless you've just become an unemployed fortune teller, that is. In which case you really should chastise yourself for not seeing it coming.

I'm not being flippant. I'm just being candid. There really is nothing the ordinary man or woman in the street could do about what's happening to our jobs. All we can do now is ride out the storm, and try to make our little corner of this recessionary world as cosy as we can.

Our strategy now is one of damage limitation; we need to try to make this recession and our brush with unemployment as pain free for ourselves and our family, as we possibly can.

Regrets, like blame, are useless emotions. They might be natural, but they serve no purpose. They don't solve anything; they don't make things better.

Worse still is feeling sorry for yourself; "Poor me; I don't deserve this, it's not fair." What kind of useless emotion is that?

I know you're disappointed about your job; so was I. I'd worked hard; I couldn't believe it when they told me I wasn't wanted anymore. The bastards; how could they do this to me?

Ok, a bit of self pity, a little anger, won't do too much harm, but don't let these feelings get out of hand and take over. Be aware, the next stop after self pity is depression; and that is to be avoided at all cost.

The most important thing to remember, when things are bad, is that shit happens. The world has never been a bed of roses. It's a rough and tumble place that can be as hard and heartless as it can be benevolent and kind. You've got to learn to take the rough with the smooth; that's the nature of things.

*"Get used to it, get over it and get on with it;"* that needs to be your motto now.

With all this doom and gloom on the jobs front, it would be easy for us all to sink into a horrible depression. Don't let that happen to you. Talk to yourself; tell yourself there are only two kinds of things: *Things you can do something about, and things you can do nothing about.* You need to learn the difference between these two imposters. You need to learn it fast, and you need to learn it now.

You can do nothing about the past; it's over. You've lost your job; that's happened. It's in the past; it's a fact. Get used to it; there's nothing you can do about it. You can't turn the clock back, stuff the words back into your boss's mouth; you can't give him back the P45 he gave you.

You can change the future though; your future. You can make it ok.

You can go down with the ship if you want to. It's your choice, but who wants to do that? Don't become a victim; victims have no future. Become a survivor; survivors live to fight another day.

Look on the bright side; think of the benefits of having some time to do all those things you've never been able to get around to. Unemployment gives you that time. It also gives you choices; and choices are something you have control over.

Remember, it's still your life; losing your job hasn't taken that away from you. You still get to make the choices; you can still make things happen. You can look for another job, or plan a holiday. You can start a new hobby, sort out the garden, go back to college, climb a mountain; join a voluntary organisation or start a small business. You can run for political office, become the President of Ireland if you want. Or you can just spend more time with your kids; that might be a nice thing to do, mightn't it.

You can do anything you want to if you put your mind to it. Honestly you can; me writing this little book is proof of that.

*'Happiness depends upon ourselves.'* - Aristotle

How you react and how you get on with life depends on your attitude; and that's something you can do something about. You can try to be positive. So you've lost your job? That's not the end of the world is it? You haven't been told you've got an incurable cancer; you're not about to die.

Anger and a desire for revenge are two other natural but equally unproductive responses to losing your job. Of course you're angry. This isn't what you wanted. It's not what you planned. You've worked hard all your life,

given it your best shot, sold your soul to the company.
You worked all the hours God gives; and this is how
you're rewarded?

Sorry, there's no sentiment in business. It's a tough, cut-
throat, mercenary world out there. It's dog eats dog; and
it's not fair. Neither is it personal; it's commercial.
Decisions are made for economic reasons. You haven't
been singled out, there's no conspiracy against you; no-
one's out to get you. There's not enough work out there
for everyone anymore. It's that simple. That's all there is
to it; facts and figures in an economic world.

So don't feel victimised; don't let anger get the better of
you. It'll only screw up your guts; give you colic and
heart burn, and make you bitter and twisted.

As for revenge? Forget it; you've much more productive
and demanding calls on your time and energy reserves
now than seeking revenge. There are far more important
things for you to be getting on with than wasting time
scheming and plotting to get even.

Shame and embarrassment are two other equally useless
and uncalled for reactions. It's amazing how we all feel
that sense of failure when we have no job. Our job
defines our standing in life. It must have something to do
with power; it certainly has nothing to do with whether
we're nice or decent people. We look up to high flyers,
solicitors, bankers, business executives; and we look
down our noses at the unemployed. And yet solicitors,

bankers, business executives, managers, even airline pilots are losing their jobs too.

Kings and queens, jokers and paupers; we're all vulnerable to the curse of unemployment. You're in good company my friend, believe me. I know of a €250,000 plus a year investment banker who's just lost his job. Let's face it; he has a lot more adjusting to life on the dole than most of us do.

OK, let's deal with the big one; fear. You've just lost your job; you're frightened. What's going to happen? How are you going to be able to cope? Will you be able to maintain your lifestyle? What about the bills, the mortgage, the school fees? Terror, panic, hysteria might start to set in if we think about all the terrible possibilities that might happen.

Unfortunately people commit suicide when they suddenly find themselves without a job and in debt. Don't do that; it's not fair to leave your mess for someone else to clear up.

Let's analyse fear. What is it? What are you frightened of? The answer's simple; you're frightened of change. Believe it or not, we're all scared of change. It's a natural response to the warm cosy complacency of something we've gotten used to. You've lost your job. Things are going to be different. How could they not be? Things are going to change and you're scared of that change, because at this moment in time you have no idea what it entails.

Let's look at it a bit differently; you're about to enter a new adventure, a new challenge. This is a new beginning. It could be really exciting, stimulating; an incredible experience that'll really make a man or woman out of you. It all depends on how you look at things, doesn't it? Is it the end of the world; or the start of a new adventure?

> *'When one door closes, another one opens.*
> *Unfortunately we often look so long at the one that's*
> *closed behind us, that we don't see the one that's been*
> *left open in front of us.'*

Who says unemployment has to be hard? Things are going to be different; that's all. The world isn't ending; the sun will still come up tomorrow morning; it'll still rain throughout most of August, and it probably won't snow at Christmas.

I'm not being flippant; change is daunting, change is scary. It means you're going to have to adapt, get used to something different; and that's means hard work. Adapting is tough; it's a challenge. It's also inconvenient; but then you're just being lazy if you think like that, aren't you?

You're frightened because you don't know what's going to happen. Fear of the unknown can be terrifying; but it's totally irrational. Why be scared of something that might never happen?

That's the whole point about the unknown; it's completely unpredictable. This could happen, that could happen, something else might happen; nothing might happen. So let's stop worrying about what might or might not happen; let's just wait and see what happens and then deal with it. It's so much easier that way, far more productive and much less stressful.

*'It is the trouble that never comes that causes the greatest loss of sleep.'*

Strange thing is, no matter what happens in life, we're always able to cope. Something crops up; it always does. That's a universal fact of life. Coping isn't the problem; adjusting is.

They say happiness is a state of mind that is able to accept what is happening. So accept what is happening in your life; you'll have a better chance of being happy.

*'Life mightn't be easy, but it is simple.'*

So you've lost your job? Stop regretting, stop resenting, stop speculating and stop worrying. It's happened; it's a done deal. The best thing you can do now is accept it. Then you'll be free to move on to whatever's meant to come next in your life.

*'The past is history, the future's a mystery.*
*All we have is the **now**; it's a gift, that's why it's called the present!'*

Oh no, I've lost my job; what am I going to do now?

# At the end of the game;

# The kings and the pawns go back in the same box.

Oh no, I've lost my job; what am I going to do now?

# TELLING FAMILY & FRIENDS
## you've become unemployed

Following hot on the heels of accepting that you have lost your job, is admitting it. Acceptance means admitting it to yourself. Admitting it to everyone else comes next, and that can be a lot more difficult.

Telling family and friends, and especially the neighbours, that you are unemployed can seem like a daunting task.

You'd be amazed at the extent some people go to try to avoid people finding out they've lost their job. I answered a phone call at work once from a woman whose husband used to work in my office. He'd been let go about 6 weeks earlier. He hadn't told anyone, not even his wife. She was phoning the office to tell her husband something important had happened to one of their children. Apparently he was leaving home every morning to go to work as usual, sandwiches and all. If the weather was good, he sat in the park until going home time. If it was raining, he went to the library. The poor woman got an awful shock when we had to explain to her that he didn't work with us anymore. I have no idea what happened when he got home that night, but my heart went out to both of them.

I know; you don't want to tell the family because you're ashamed. You're a proud person; you feel a failure, you've let them down. You don't want to burden them, you don't want them to worry. The best advice I can give is tell them immediately. They've a right to know. You losing your job will affect them almost as much as it affects you. They need to know the effect it's going to have on them. They need to adjust their lifestyle, cut back. They need to spend less. They have a right to know.

Tell them you've lost your job. Tell them you are upset about this, but it's not the end of the world. Explain things will need to be different. There will be less money, but you're not going to starve or lose your house and nothing dreadful is going to happen. Reassure them that if you're all sensible and adjust your spending then everything will work out ok.

Don't be overly apologetic as you tell them, you've done nothing wrong. Losing your job is not a crime, it's not a sin; you can't go to prison for it. Neither is it a black mark on your CV. It's something that can happen to anybody; nobody's job is safe anymore. Make sure the family understands this.

Teenage children can find it particularly hard if their parent loses his or her job. They may be reluctant to tell their friends or social circle. Discuss this with them; explain it isn't a social stigma to lose your job anymore. Be understanding if they feel embarrassed or ashamed though; and don't take it personally. They are at a vulnerable stage in their lives, blending in with the crowd and keeping up appearances are important to them.

If other members of the family are working, tell them they are the lucky ones and remind them how valuable jobs are these days; but don't put pressure on them so they think they have to keep their job at all costs. Don't prepare them for a guilt trip if they have the misfortune to lose their job in the future.

Coping with a problem on your own is far harder than sharing it with someone else. It may seem unfair to burden other people with your difficulties; but isn't that what families are supposed to be all about? Let's be honest, wouldn't you prefer they told you if they were in trouble, rather than keeping it from you? Wouldn't you prefer if your partner, or your son or daughter, told you they'd lost their job, rather than pretending otherwise?

*'A problem shared is a problem halved.*
*There's no problem so big, that it can't be solved over a cup of tea.'*

As for the neighbours, or other members of the golf club, or your mates in the pub? Tell them too. They'll find out soon enough anyway. They'll notice the change in your routine. Better to come out straight and tell them, than have them speculating about you behind your back. Don't worry; it probably won't be long before one of them loses his job too, if that hasn't happened already.

Telling other people that you've lost your job is good therapy. It helps you get used to the idea and adjust to your new reality. Putting off the evil day just prolongs the agony and leads to all kinds of lies, deceits and cover ups.

You'd be surprised too how willing people are to help. In my opinion the Celtic Tiger destroyed one of Ireland's traditional strengths, neighbourliness. Everyone has been so busy chasing the Tiger's tail; the courtesies that Ireland was famous for have disappeared behind high wrought iron fences, security gates, CCTV and intercoms. The time to chat and help out neighbours and friends got swamped in a sea of 4x4's, fake tans, IPODs, designer labels and road rage.

They say every cloud has a silver lining. Maybe this recession will give us back the Ireland that we once knew and loved; some good must surely come out of all this doom and gloom.

So tell the neighbours, tell your friends, tell the dogs in the street; you've lost your job, but that doesn't mean you've lost your dignity. You're still the same person you always were.

Oh and don't have any truck with that 'Poor Mr. Murphy has lost his job,' rubbish. You're not poor Mr Murphy; you're not poor Mr. Anybody. You're lucky. You've got choices. You've got a new range of options open to you. You've new challenges to contend with.

Depending how you look at things, your life has just got much more interesting now that you've lost your job. Be cheerful, be upbeat, stay proud, and help put a stop to the awful judgement that people have traditionally aimed at the unemployed.

*'But for the grace of God, go I.'*

You've lost your job; you're unemployed. You're disappointed, you're apprehensive; you're unsure what's going to happen next. Of course you are; you're human. Nobody expects you to be Superman.

You've lost your job; you're unemployed. You can't do much about that can you, except accept it.

Go on admit it to yourself. Say it out loud, **"I've lost my job! I'm unemployed!"**

Say it again, only this time slowly and more quietly, **"I've lost my job. I'm unemployed; but it's ok; I'll manage!"**

*'When the going gets tough; the tough get going!'*

Oh no, I've lost my job; what am I going to do now?

# It's only money!

Oh no, I've lost my job; what am I going to do now?

# FINANCIAL CONSIDERATIONS

Let's face it; the most immediate consequence of losing your job is going to be a financial one. You're going to have less money, possibly a lot less money, than you've been used to.

Everybody's financial position is different. Everyone is going to have to work out their own situation and take appropriate steps to keep their finances under control. Everyone's solution will be different.

This recession is no respecter of status or tradition. Unemployment might once have been the curse of the lower classes. Not anymore. The present economic crisis is affecting every walk of life. Blue collar, white collar, middle manager, executive, public sector employee; no-one's job is safe anymore. Estimates suggest over half a million people might have lost their jobs in Ireland by the end of 2009. Most of those will never have been unemployed before. This is going to be an experience very few of us are prepared for.

It's a horrible feeling, having no money; especially if you've been used to a regular and reasonable income. For people who've never been without before, living on subsistence levels, which is really what life on the dole is like, is going to be hard.

It's not that you won't be able to afford the basics like food. It's not the expensive things you're going to miss. It's the little luxuries and treats that make life fun and enjoyable. They can no longer be permitted; and they are going to be most missed. Taking the kids to the cinema and buying popcorn, coffee in Starbucks, the odd take away, a night in with a bottle of wine and a few DVDs, a night out with the girls or the lads, a weekend break; all these things are going to become off limits.

Whereas you used to buy things without thinking; now you're going to have to evaluate everything before you allow yourself to spend. You'll be constantly thinking, "Can I afford this?" More often than not, the answer will be, "No I can't, I'll have to do without."

I remember standing outside Easons for 10 minutes debating whether I could afford a €12.75 book. I wanted it for research I was doing to help me write this little book. I felt stupid and pathetic. A paperback book for pity's sake; and me worrying whether I could justify spending €12.75 to buy it? In the end I bought it. Making that decision said as much about my confidence that I would be able to survive this recession as anything else.

Sudden, unplanned expenses are going to be a nightmare. The car or washing machine breaking down can easily throw everything else off balance. The kid's coming home and telling you about a school trip they want to go on. How are you going to tell them you can't afford it?

It is important that you learn to budget; and that almost certainly entails making sacrifices. I started swimming as a way of keeping fit while I was working. I had to stop after I lost my job. Two swims a week cost €15. A bag of coal costs €17. It's winter; so the coal wins.

I'm not trying to paint an unnecessarily bleak picture. I just want you to realise it's going to be tough being without a job. There will be no more pay cheques at the end of the week or month to clear the overdraft, or pay off the credit cards.

Now that you're unemployed, you are going to have to start dealing in cash. If the money isn't in your pocket, you can't spend it. It's as simple as that.

*'Spend only what you have, don't spend what you haven't got.'*

Above all, don't be tempted to borrow to finance things you can't pay for; not unless it is absolutely necessary and you are sure you will be able to pay it back. NEVER BE TEMPTED TO BORROW FROM UNLICENSED MONEY LENDERS. They charge exorbitant interest rates and have few scruples when it comes to collecting what they are owed.

A word of hope; living on the dole is much worse at the very beginning, but it does get better when things settle down.

Losing your job can be like being in the shower when the water supply suddenly gets turned off. You're covered in soap suds but there's no water to rinse you off.

If your income suddenly stops, it can be a while before all the bills, commitments and promises can be brought under control. The overdraft and credit card balances, that were no problem when you were working, suddenly seem like a mountain to climb when your only income is the dole. The holiday, Holy Communion, 21$^{st}$ party or whatever it was you committed to when you were working looms like Armageddon now your income is only a quarter of what it was.

You may have to contend with more than just losing your wages or salary when your job has gone. If you're a salesman, you might lose your car. If you're a tradesman, you might lose your tools. If you're a manager, you might lose your laptop. The problem is you mightn't have the where-with-all to replace them.

In my own case I lost my car, phone and laptop. I live in the country; the nearest shop is 5 miles away, the dole office is 10 miles away. It was tough getting about. I found not having access to the internet particularly hard.

I got through it though; just as you will. It gets better, after you have things under control

*'Hope springs eternal.'*

The next few sub-chapters aim to give you the guidelines to resolving your financial position now you've become unemployed.

Before we get into the ins and outs of budgets, mortgages, credit cards, and all that kind of stuff; let's make three things absolutely clear:

- You are not going to be destitute
- You are not going to starve, neither are your family
- You are not going to be homeless

Thank God we live in a Western European society. We have a social welfare and health system that will look after us. It mightn't be perfect, but it's still a blessing that we should all be grateful for. We should thank our lucky stars we live in Ireland and not an impoverished third world country where people starve for the want of bowl of rice.

Don't be worrying unduly about money; God, or in this case the State, really will provide.

In the next few sub-chapters we'll take a look at what to do to sort your finances out under the following headings:

- Getting Spending Under Control
- Benefits, Assistance and Entitlements
- Dealing with Borrowings
- What about Savings?

Oh no, I've lost my job; what am I going to do now?

# GETTING SPENDING UNDER CONTROL

By now, I'm sure you realise things are going to be different now you're unemployed; but what does different mean?

In simple terms, it means you're not going to be able to spend as much money as you've been used to. That might seem like a bit of an obvious statement. You'd be surprised though, how many people carry on spending as if nothing's happened; particularly if they've got a bit of cash in their pocket or a few quid in their current account. Even worse, some people go on a spending spree and run up their overdraft or credit cards to the max. Others go mad and spend their redundancy cheque on an exotic holiday or a fancy new car. I even heard of one couple who spent their lump-sum on a lavish 25th wedding anniversary party. Good luck to them, I suppose; but I wouldn't recommend splashing the cash in the current economic climate.

Spending your redundancy money or your savings, or money you don't have, is a kind of 'let's enjoy it while we can and sod the consequences' response to losing your job. In some ways it is understandable if it helps get over the depression associated with becoming unemployed.

The problem is, once money is spent, it's gone. It can't be got back; it's gone forever. The best advice after you lose your job therefore, is; hold on to your money, make it last as long as you possibly can.

There's something else about spending. It might be you that lost your job, but it probably isn't you that does the bulk of the spending. Take an honest look at your household. Who is spending the money? You'll be surprised, everybody's spending, your partner, the kids; as well as you. Controlling spending means making everybody in the household aware that things are different now; everyone's going to have to adjust and cut back on their spending.

When you're reviewing spending, you need to bear in mind that the younger generation, (that probably means everybody under 25), grew up with the Celtic Tiger. They aren't used to having no money. They've always had pretty much whatever they've wanted. Adjusting the spending expectations of the younger members of your family is going to be difficult, but it is essential if you are going to survive unemployment.

It's not just cash spending that you need to look at. All those standing orders and direct debits have got to be reviewed too; the golf club membership, the satellite TV subscription, and the mobile phone accounts. They're all hidden forms of spending that frequently get forgotten when people ask, "Where does all our money go?"

Repaying loans is often the biggest expenditure in a household budget. You might think there's nothing you can do about them; they're a fixed cost. They might be taking up all your income, but you'll just have to put up with them. You're wrong; loans can be refinanced, payments can be rescheduled. They're just as much a part of spending as the grocery shopping, the phone bill or the electricity bill; and they need to be reviewed too.

You might be surprised that I'm focusing on spending first, rather than discussing income. There are two reasons for this:

- Firstly, I want you to realise that even though you are unemployed, you're still in control of your finances. Losing your job is not a doomsday scenario; you don't have to hand over your life and your affairs, and meekly surrender to whatever fate has in store for you. You mightn't have a job anymore, but you're still in the driving seat; you can sort things out. You can make unemployment a good or a bad experience for you and your family. It depends on how you adjust; and the biggest adjustment you've got to make is? You guessed it, spending.

- Secondly, when you first become unemployed your future income is almost certainly unknown. It usually takes a while to get benefits sorted out; and they will usually be back dated to the day you became unemployed. Money spent on the other hand is gone; it can't be back dated or clawed back. Controlling spending will have an immediate benefit. Cutting costs should never be delayed; it is something you can and should do right away.

Let's underline one simple fact: getting spending under control is essential if you are to prosper whilst being unemployed.

So how do you go about getting spending under control?

As with everything, you must first find out where you're starting from. That means making a list of everything you currently spend and what you spend it on.

"Oh no," I can you hear you groaning; "Not a list; I hate lists."

Sorry folks, a written list of everything you spend is absolutely essential. Why? Because 99% of us don't have a clue what we spend our money on; but we need to find out if we're going to take control of our finances.

You're going to be amazed when you finish making your spending list. I can hear you now exclaiming your surprise at where all your money's been going. "I forgot all about that standing order. I never realised we spent so much on take-away meals. Do we really spend all that on a Saturday night out? Can you believe we spent that much on taxis? Has make-up got that expensive? God my hairdresser's been doing well out of me these last few years! Is that how much video games cost? Do I really spend all that on cigarettes? I can't believe I've spent that much playing golf."

Take the preparation of your spending list seriously. Don't rush it. Don't guess what things cost; find out. If you don't know what you're spending your money on, start a spending log. Jot down every penny you spend over a two or four week period, and make that the basis of your spending list.

Your spending list needs to be long; it needs to be comprehensive and it needs to honestly reflect where all your money's been going.

Time spent preparing your spending list really will be worth it, because:

- You aren't going to have as much money to spend as you used to have.
- Something's got to give and you've got to chose what that something is.
- It is far better to have a plan than no idea what you're going to do now you've less income.
- It'll give you heart, when you see how much money you've been spending and wasting, that surviving unemployment isn't going to be as hard as you first thought it would be.

Involve all the family in making the spending list. Let them see where the money's being spent; they're going to have to help to cut it back. Oh and listen to them when you discuss ways of saving money; their views are important.

Compile the list in sections. Decide on a period (e.g. weekly or monthly). Put the amount for the period against each item of expenditure.

A template for a possible listing is presented below:

- Regular Outgoings:
    o Rent
    o Electricity
    o Gas
    o Heating Oil
    o Coal Merchant
    o Life Assurance
    o Pension
    o Saving Schemes
    o Medical Insurance
    o Building & Contents Insurance
    o Car Insurance
    o Bin Charges
    o Satellite and Cable TV
    o Telephone Bills - ( land lines, mobiles and internet)
- Fixed Loan Repayments:
    o Mortgage
    o Car Loans
    o Hire Purchase Agreements (e.g. furniture, washing machine, TV, computer etc)
    o Other Personal Loans
- Variable Loan Repayments:
    o Credit Card(s) – List them all
    o Store Card(s) – List them all
    o Overdraft Repayments
- Other Regular Payments:
    o Membership Subscriptions – List them all
    o Magazine or Journal Subscriptions – List them all
    o Charitable Donations
- Education Costs:
    o College and School Fees
    o Travelling & Accommodation Costs
- Child Related Costs:
    o Allowances & Pocket Money

- o Activities – (dancing lessons, horse riding, youth clubs etc)
  - o Child Minding
  - o Baby Sitting
- Housekeeping Costs:
  - o Groceries:
  - o Milkman
  - o Newsagent
- Motoring Costs – List separately for each vehicle:
  - o Fuel
  - o Repairs & Maintenance
  - o Road Tax
  - o Insurance
  - o Break Down Service
  - o Car Wash & Valletting
  - o Car Parking Charges
- Public Transport
  - o Buses
  - o Trains
  - o Luas
  - o Taxis
  - o Flights
- Discretionary Expenditure:
  - o Clothing
  - o Cosmetics
  - o Hobbies
  - o CDs, DVDs, Games, Downloads
- Entertaining & Socialising:
  - o Alcohol
  - o Cigarettes
  - o Cinema, Theatre
  - o Eating Out
- Holidays & Weekend Breaks
- Services:
  - o Home Cleaning
  - o Window Cleaning
  - o Garden Maintenance
- Other Costs:
  - o Second Home?
  - o Time Share?
  - o Contribution to elderly person's home help or nursing home?
- Etc, etc, etc.

Wow, that's a long list! Scary isn't it, to sit down and take a long hard look at what you've been spending all your money on?

Add everything up – now you're really in shock. Could you really be spending that much each week/month?

That was the easy part. Now comes the time for tough decisions. Go back over your list and prune it back; go over it once, go over it twice, go over it three times. Be vigilant; ask yourself and your family:
- Is this expense really necessary?
- Do we really have to spend all of it?
- Could we save some of it?
- Could we do it less often?
- Could we postpone it and come back to it when things improve?
- Could we manage without it altogether?"

## Some practical tips to help you save money:
- Make a shopping list before you go to the shops.
- Buy only what you need when you're shopping.
- Shop carefully. Shop around and compare prices.
- Ask for a discount; you'll be amazed how many shops will give you a bit off
- Look out for bargains, but avoid spontaneous purchases
- Supermarket own label products are often cheaper than heavily advertised brands
- Many supermarkets have 'value lines' that are particularly low cost
- Buy fresh, rather than processed, food; it's cheaper and better for you
- Switch to packed lunches rather than sandwich bars or delis
- Buy in bulk when you can

- By second hand when you can
- Smoke less, or better still give up
- Accessorise rather than buy more clothes
- Try ebay for bargains
- Use store loyalty cards; it's great to get a few euro back in vouchers
- Don't throw good things away; sell them on ebay or give to a charity shop
- Don't use store credit cards; they usually have very high interest rates
- Do it yourself rather than pay for tradesmen
- Keep the duration of phone calls to a minimum
- Text rather than call
- Use e-mail or Skype for long distance communication
- Turn off lights when you are not in a room. Do you really need to have every light on in the house?
- Turn down the heating; wear an extra jumper
- Lag the hot water cylinder; it'll repay itself within a year
- Don't leave the hot tap running
- Avoid electric fires
- Take a look in your freezer. What's in it? (It costs a lot of money to keep an out of date pizza frozen for 2 years)
- Use the tumble dryer sparingly
- Turn off appliances at night (not fridge or freezer); leaving them on standby wastes money
- Wash clothes less often; get a couple of wears out of them
- Shower rather than bathe, but don't spend too long in the shower
- Don't overfill the kettle
- Trade the car down for a smaller, more efficient one
- Use the car less often;
- Avoid taxis; use public transport instead
- Travel off peak; it's usually cheaper
- Walk or cycle whenever you can
- Renegotiate insurances

A couple of thoughts to help you with your spending evaluation programme. Be realistic; you can't live on air alone, so set priorities. Basic needs must be met before luxuries. It doesn't make sense to starve the kids, just so you can play a round of golf, or go on a fancy holiday.

When you're reviewing your list; mortgages, loans, credit cards and other borrowings can seem like an insurmountable millstone around your neck. They don't have to be. Don't worry if you can't afford them; they can be renegotiated. Write down what you think you can afford to repay alongside each item. It'll do as a starting point to considering what to do about each loan. We'll look as this area in more detail in a later chapter.

Put your proposed saving alongside each item. Discuss and agree the savings with the relevant members of your family. Now add up all the savings; feels good doesn't it to think you can save all that money.

Sit back, have a cup of tea; you've earned it. Oh and congratulations, you've just taken your first step to surviving unemployment.

# BENEFITS, ASSISTANCE AND ENTITLEMENTS

"What are my entitlements? How much am I going to get?"

For some people that's the first question that goes through their mind when they lose their job. For others the thought of having to go on the dole is horrifying.

Before we look at what and how much you might be entitled to, let's dwell on that word entitlement for a moment or two.

Entitlement means just that; it is something you are entitled to; a right you are permitted to claim without any consequence or consideration. It is yours as a matter of basic principle.

You are entitled to claim the dole or any other benefit because you are a member of our society. You have paid your contributions through income tax, PRSI, VAT on everything you ever bought, road tax, fuel tax, excise duty on alcohol and cigarettes, stamp duty on your house and so on and so on and so on.

It might also surprise you to know that virtually everybody in Ireland receives benefits of some kind or another.

Over a third of the population depends solely or partly on maintenance payments. About the same number get health services paid for by the State. Every child in the land benefits from Child Allowance. More than a quarter of the population are benefitting from subsidised education. Almost every home in the country has been purchased with the help of tax relief on the mortgage.

So if you're one of those proud people who think it would be wrong to claim social welfare benefit; cop on to yourself. You, like all the rest of us, are entitled to it. Social welfare benefits are yours by right. They are not hand outs, they're not charity; they're not beneath your dignity. You have as much right to them as you do to ride on a subsidised bus, or drive around the M50 or visit the National Museum of Ireland.

Apply for what you are entitled to, and join the thousands of construction workers, nurses, bankers, factory workers, lorry drivers, teachers, businessmen, publicans, single parents, bar maids, solicitors, shop workers, old age pensioners and council employees who are claiming their rights too.

You might find it a bit daunting when you first visit the Social Welfare Office. It will probably be very busy and crowded. There is also very little privacy. Don't be put off; everyone there is in the same boat as you are. Some offices will have a sequential ticketing system; others will have an informal queuing system, a bit like a doctor's waiting room.

When it comes to your turn, explain to the Social Welfare Officer that you've lost your job. They will take you through the rest of the procedure and will probably get you to fill in a registration form.

My experience of my local Social Welfare Office was a good one. Everybody I came into contact with was friendly, understanding and helpful. So don't be shy, don't be embarrassed and don't be ashamed; no-one in the welfare office is going to bite.

**Employed or Self- Employed** - Before we start looking at what you might be entitled to, we need to distinguish between two different types of employment. Your entitlements will depend on whether you were working as an employee or were self-employed.

Determining what type of employment applies to you may be more complicated than you imagine. Many employers describe workers as self-employed or contractors when they are actually employees. It is not your job title, job description or contract of employment that determines whether you are an employee or are self-employed; it is the way you work that matters. If you work regular hours, get regular payments, provide labour only and don't provide tools or equipment, can't sub-contract what you do and are not a separate business, then you are probably an employee; even if you have been described by your employer as self employed.

Employees are protected by Labour Laws and have rights to redundancy, sick pay and so on which self-employed people don't have. If you have any doubt about your status, see the chapter on Seeking Help.

Remember it will probably be to your advantage to establish that you are an employee rather than self–employed.

One other area that often creates confusion is the difference between full time and part time employees. Generally speaking there is no difference to the rights and entitlements of part-time workers compared to full time workers.

**EMPLOYEES** - The following information relates to employees:

**Notice Period** - When you lose your job, the first thing you must check is that you have received sufficient notice. The minimum notice period depends on length of continuous service, in other words how long you have been with your current employer.

Minimum notice periods are as follows:

| | |
|---|---|
| 13 weeks to less than 2 years service – | One week's notice |
| 2 years to less than 5 years service - | Two week's notice |
| 5 years to less than 10 years service - | Four week's notice |
| 10 years to less than 15 years service- | Six week's notice |
| More than 15 years service- | Eight week's notice |

If you think your period of notice may have been wrong, contact the Employment Appeals Tribunal; (see the chapter on Seeking Help).

**Redundancy** - You may also be entitled to a redundancy payment. A redundancy situation arises when an employee's job no longer exists and he or she is not being replaced. You may be entitled to redundancy if your employer is closing down or cutting back on staff numbers.

To qualify for a redundancy payment you must be employed (full or part-time) and have at least two years (104 weeks) continuous service with your present employer.

If you qualify, you are entitled to a minimum lump sum payment calculated as two weeks pay for every year of continuous service plus a bonus week added on. Your pay means your gross pay and is currently subject to a ceiling of €600 per week. In other words, if you earn more than €600 per week, your minimum redundancy entitlement will be calculated as though you only earned €600 per week. Your employer may opt to pay more than the minimum. Lump sum redundancy payments up to the ceiling of €600 per week are tax free.

As an example, if you have been working with your employer for 15 years and your current gross pay is €500 per week; you are entitled to receive a minimum lump sum redundancy payment of 31 weeks (15 x 2 = 30 + 1 = 31) at €500, which amounts to €15,500.

Redundancy payments are made by your employer. If your employer can't pay them, then the Social Insurance Fund administered by the Department of Enterprise, Trade and Employment covers them.

If you think you should have been entitled to a Redundancy Payment or that your lump sum calculation is wrong, contact the Employment Appeals Tribunal (see the chapter on Seeking Help).

**Holiday Pay** – When you leave employment you are entitled to receive any unpaid holiday pay. The general rule is you are entitled to a minimum of 4 weeks holiday pay, (in addition to public holidays), in a 12 month period. If you have worked less than 12 months your holiday entitlement is reduced accordingly.

Check to make sure you have received the correct amount of unpaid holiday pay when you are leaving your employment. See the chapter on Seeking Help if you think your holiday pay was calculated incorrectly.

**Tax Refunds** – You may be entitled to a tax refund when you become unemployed. This could arise because the PAYE system deducts tax throughout the year on the assumption that your income will continue at the same level until the year end. Ask your Inspector of Taxes for a Form P50 to claim back any tax due.

**Unemployment Benefits** – You are entitled to receive unemployment benefit if you are:
- Unemployed
- Or have suffered a considerable loss of work
- Capable of work
- Available to work
- Genuinely seeking work
- Aged under 65

You may also have to prove you are normally resident in Ireland.

Two different types of benefit are available depending on your particular circumstances:

- **Job Seeker's Benefit** is paid to those who satisfy certain PRSI conditions. For new claimants, that generally means they have 2 years (104 weeks) paid PRSI contributions. The amount of payment you receive will be linked to your age and amount of PRSI paid. It could be up to €204 per week for a single person.

- **Job Seeker's Allowance** is a means-tested payment available to people who don't satisfy the PRSI conditions associated with the Job Seeker's Benefit. Means-testing simply means your financial situation is assessed to see if you genuinely need assistance. This is normally done at an interview with a Social Welfare Inspector. Don't be put off by the title 'Inspector'; it's just someone whose job is to check you aren't a millionaire, but a genuine case of someone who is unemployed and needs financial assistance. You will be asked to provide information about your savings, any assets you may own (e.g. property, shares), yours and your partner's income. The amount of payment you receive will be linked to your means. It could be up to €204 per week for a single person.

To apply for either Job Seeker's Benefit or Job Seeker's Allowance you need to register at your local Social Welfare Office. You can find their address in the phone book.

Register on the first day you become unemployed; do not delay. Bring your P45 and recent P60, bank details, passport or birth certificate with you. If you don't have these documents with you, register anyway and provide them at a later date.

Remember delaying your registration will only delay receipt of your benefit payments.

**SELF EMPLOYED PERSONS** – The rules for self employed people are different. You are still entitled to receive the Job Seeker's Allowance, subject of course to your means being assessed. Register with your local Social Welfare Office immediately you have no work. They will then discuss your benefit options with you. The amount of payment you receive will be linked to your means. It could be up to €204 per week for a single person.

**OTHER BENEFITS** – In addition to unemployment benefit, you may be entitled to receive other benefits depending on your particular financial circumstances:

- **One Parent Family Payment** is available to men and women bringing up a child or children without the help of a partner.

- **Family Income Supplement** is available to help families on low incomes where at least one member of the family is working. So if your partner is still working and receiving a low income, after you lose your job, you may be eligible for this payment.

- **Supplementary Welfare Allowance** is available to people with no or very little income. This may be the situation if you are waiting for other benefits to be processed. If, for whatever reasons you find yourself with no money, or with an essential bill (e.g. ESB bill) you cannot pay; you should apply for help under this scheme.

- **Mortgage Interest Supplement** is available if you are unable to meet your mortgage repayments. It is subject to a means test. If you qualify, it only pays the interest not the capital portion of your repayments.

- **Rent Supplement** is available to people who have been assessed by the Housing Authority as being in need of a house. It may also be available if you are living in private rented accommodation (not local authority housing) and are unable to pay your rent. It is means tested.

- **Medical Card** – If you are receiving means tested benefits you may also be entitled to a medical card.

To apply for the **One Parent Family Payment** or **Family Income Supplement** you need to contact your local **Social Welfare Office** (see your local phone book).

To apply for the **Supplementary Welfare Allowance, Mortgage Interest Supplement, Rent Allowance** or a **Medical Card** contact your local **Health Office of health centre** (see your local phone book).

# DEALING WITH BORROWINGS AND DEBTS

Dealing with borrowings and debts can be a major headache if you unexpectedly lose your job and your income suddenly drops. It is critical that you don't hide or run away from your debts. Ignoring reminder letters is the worst possible thing you can do. The important thing is to face up to your changed situation and take action.

Whilst you were working you may have had everything paid up to date. You mightn't have considered yourself to be 'in debt'. Alternatively you may have been in arrears; maybe you thought of yourselves as 'up to my in ears in debt'.

Whatever your situation, it is important to realise that any money you owe is a debt. Even if your mortgage and other loans are up to date, the balances still remaining to be paid are debts. Your changed situation could mean you won't be able to keep up repayments in the future.

So don't skip this chapter just because you're up to date with your payments.

Debts come in many shapes and sizes. They include:
- A mortgage
- A second mortgage
- Personal loans, for example for a car
- An overdraft

- Hire purchase agreements for furniture, a TV or a washing machine
- Credit cards
- Store Cards
- A secured loan, for example a business loan
- Loans from a family member or friend
- Unpaid medical or educational bills
- Unpaid tax liabilities

Everybody's financial circumstances are different. A person's financial situation is as unique as his or her face. Your debts may be small and easily managed, or they may be huge and complicated. You may have savings, or have been fortunate enough to receive a redundancy payment that can be offset against what you owe. You might have guaranteed a business loan. Your assets might be at risk of being repossessed by your creditors. You might have taken out insurance against a debt or against loss of income. All of these points will impact on what you need to do to resolve your debt situation.

It is impossible to generalise. The solution to one person or family's debt predicament may be completely wrong for someone else's.

Some simple steps are relevant to everyone though:

- Firstly, take stock of your debts -
  - Make a list of everything you owe
  - Find out how much is still remaining to be paid

- o Add up the total amount still remaining to be paid on all your debts – this is your indebtedness
- o Write down the interest rate you are paying against each debt
- o Write down the required repayment and frequency (weekly/monthly) against each debt
- o Add up the total amount of your repayments each period
- Secondly, work out how much you can comfortably afford to pay towards your borrowings after you have paid for your necessary bills such as food, electricity and so on.
- Thirdly, compare what you are supposed to pay against what you can afford to pay.

Maybe you can manage to keep paying your debts. If not what is the shortfall each period? Is it large or is it small?

If the shortfall between what you are supposed to pay and what you can afford to pay each period is small, it may be prudent to consider extending some of your loans over a slightly longer period, thereby reducing the amount that has to be paid each week/month. If this is the case it would be important to consider extending those loans with the lowest interest rates (for example the mortgage) rather than the higher rate borrowings like credit cards and overdrafts. The quicker you can pay off the higher rate loans the better, because they are costing you the most money to service. So if you need to extend the period of your borrowing to reduce your monthly repayments, try to extend the low rate ones rather than high rate ones.

If the shortfall between what you can afford to pay each month and what you are supposed to pay is large, then it may be sensible to consider refinancing or consolidating all your loans into one. This means borrowing enough from one source to pay everybody else back. Once again it would be important to borrow from a low rate source such as a secured loan, rather than a high rate source like a credit card or overdraft.

Consolidating your loans into one will generally be much easier if you own a house as this can be used for security.

Some debts, for example an overdraft, or the taxman, don't have a repayment period and need to be paid immediately. Other debts may be seriously in arrears and also need urgent attention.

Three options may be available to resolve these types of debts. You could agree a payment plan, which means agreeing to pay a fixed amount each week, or month, until the full debt is repaid. The lender might agree to write off part of the balance if you are able to pay the remainder as a lump sum. Alternatively, large amounts might be able to be repaid by remortgaging your home.

Whatever course of action seems appropriate, it is important that you contact everybody you owe money to and explain your situation. Even if you think you can keep paying everybody, it would still be beneficial to let them know your situation has changed.

I suggest sending a letter like this (* use whichever is appropriate):

> Dear Sir,
> Unfortunately I have recently *lost my job/been made redundant** and I now find myself unemployed.
> I am registering with the Department of Social Welfare for unemployment benefit; this may take a couple of weeks to be sorted out.
> In the meantime I am writing to you to explain that
> - *I am not in a position to make any payment until my unemployment benefits are resolved and would therefore request a payment break for xx weeks/months**
> - *I need to make reduced payments of €xx each week/month for a period of xx weeks/months**
> - *I need to make an appointment to see you to discuss my situation**
>
> I thank you for your understanding in this matter
>
> Yours faithfully,

You will obviously receive a reply to your letter. This will probably be via a telephone call. Don't be alarmed when you get the call; you have already put the lender on notice that your circumstances have changed and that you want to resolve the situation. You will be surprised how willing they will be in helping you sort things out.

One source of help may be your local bank, or perhaps your local credit union. Make an appointment to meet them, even if you don't owe them money. Explain your circumstances and ask if they are able to help you.

*'If you don't ask; you don't get.'*

When dealing with banks, building societies, credit card companies etc; you must remember, they make money by lending money. They don't make money on what you pay them back; they make it on what you owe them. As long as you are talking to them and making a genuine effort to pay them what you can afford they will be ok. They will still be earning their interest and making a profit out of you.

What worries them is the risk of a bad debt; if that happens they lose their money and their profit suffers.

What frightens banks, building societies and other lenders, and makes them come after you, is not hearing from you or receiving no payments from you over a prolonged period of time. So don't avoid or ignore them. Tell them what is happening. Discuss your situation with them. That way a mutually agreeable solution can be found.

One important point to keep in mind if you can't pay your debts is; "Blood can't be got from a stone."

So don't worry unduly if you genuinely can't afford to repay a debt. Faced with a situation, where there is little or no chance of collecting the debt, banks and credit card companies will eventually write off the amount that's due. This will affect your future ability to borrow though, as you will be registered as a bad payer with a credit bureau.

Woe betides you though, if you have income, savings or assets but can't be bothered, or make no effort, to pay your debts. In such cases, the lender could seek a Court Order requiring you to pay.

You can no longer go to prison for debt, but you can if you fail to obey a Court Order. So, if the Judge says pay, and you don't; you could end up behind bars.

Your savings and assets could also be taken from you to pay off what you owe. This would require a Court Order, which the lender will normally be able to get. Assets secured against a loan are obviously at risk.

Cars, vans, boats and so on that are subject to hire purchase agreements can be repossessed by the lender. They are usually then sold at auction, which means they don't fetch a very good price. What they do fetch is offset against the amount of your debt. You then owe what's left; and the lender will come looking for that.

Other assets that you own can be seized by the Sherriff, following a Court Order, and used to pay off your debts.

Once again, they will usually be sold cheaply at auction. The proceeds will then be offset against what you owe. If this happens, not only will you have lost your asset, you'll still owe the remainder of the balance due.

It is obviously far better to come to an arrangement to pay your debts, than have Court Orders against you, assets seized, and even face the prospect of imprisonment for not obeying a Court Order to pay.

*'Jaw jaw is better than war war!'* Winston Churchill

**Family Home** – the position regarding the family home is complex. The Family Home Protection Act confers certain protections, for example that one spouse cannot sell, mortgage or dispose of the home without the other spouse's consent; but this only applies to married couples. It doesn't protect non-married partners. In simple terms, where one spouse gives a personal guarantee for a loan, the family home would be safe unless the other spouse had consented to it being offered as security against the loan.

In the case of a mortgage secured on a home, both spouses would normally have consented to the security, so your home could be at risk if you default on your mortgage repayments. However banks and building societies are reluctant to repossess the family home and would normally work with you to reschedule the debt.

Remember, whatever your financial situation, don't panic, don't hide or run away, don't ignore reminder or warning letters. Take action and take it now. Contact the lender, tell them the truth about your situation and discuss with them how best to resolve it.

**If you need help deciding what to do about your debts contact your local MABS office.**

MABS, the Money Advice and Budgetary Service, is a free and confidential service for people in debt or about to go into debt. They can be found in your local phone book.

Don't forget to join the Job Seekers Union; they are self help group for people who've lost their jobs. You can find them at www.thejobseekersunion.com

Oh no, I've lost my job; what am I going to do now?

# WHAT ABOUT SAVINGS?

Savings are for when you fall on hard times. They are money put aside for the time when it might be needed.

"Put a bit by for a rainy day" is an old saying that makes a lot of sense.

I remember one lady telling me her old mother had advised her to always keep some *running away money* hidden somewhere. I guess in her mother's day, before equality, it was probably prudent for a woman to have her *running away money*; just in case the husband turned nasty.

Hopefully the days of *running away money* are long gone, but if you have savings how wise and fortunate you are.

How should you use your savings if you've just lost your job and your income isn't what it used to be? Should you dip into them to subsidise your expenditure? Should you use them to pay off all or some of your debts? Or you should you hang on to them in case things get worse?

The answer to all those questions is the same; it depends.

It depends on how large your savings are. It depends how old you are. It depends what your future commitments, for things like education or retirement, are going to be.

What to do with your savings is too big of a subject for generalisations; and it most certainly isn't a question you should be in any rush to answer.

My simple advice to the person with savings would be:
- Wait as long can before you spend them;
- And then spend them as slowly as you can.

Remember, it is quite likely we are going to enter a period of deflation. That means things will get cheaper rather than more expensive over time. If that happens, your savings will become more valuable as each day passes, because they will be able to buy more things tomorrow than would have been able to buy today.

So hang on to your savings if you can. In this recessionary climate, a bird in the hand really is worth two in the bush.

One word of caution though, many people's savings are under threat as stock market and commodity prices crash.

It would do no harm, if you have savings, to consult a professional advisor to ensure your savings are protected; but talk over the professional's advice with a friend or family member who you trust before you accept it; and if you're not sure get a second opinion.

**Pick yourself up,**

**Dust yourself down;**

**And start all over again.**

**Oh no, I've lost my job; what am I going to do now?**

# LOOKING FOR ANOTHER JOB

Before we start to consider how to go about finding another job, I think we should be realistic. Getting a job in today's economic climate isn't going to be easy; there aren't as many opportunities out there as there used to be.

But that doesn't mean there are none, and it doesn't mean you shouldn't try. There are still vacancies, lots of them; but you may have to be prepared to lower your sights a little from where they used to be set.

**Looking for a job is a job in itself** – If you want a job, you must be prepared to have to work hard at finding it.

You're going to have to approach job hunting as a project in itself; and like all projects you need to prepare a project plan.

Your project plan to find a new job needs to include the following:
- Preparing your CV
- Registering your details with recruitment websites like loadzajobs.ie
- Registering with local and specialised recruitment agencies
- Regularly browsing the recruitment websites
- Regularly visiting your local FAS office to review vacancies

- Regularly reviewing the local newspaper for vacancies
- Regularly reviewing the national newspapers for vacancies
- Giving your CV to local businesses
- Sending out speculative CV's to promote yourself
- Keeping a Job Hunters journal
- Keeping yourself busy whilst you are looking for a job

**Preparing your CV** – The Curriculum Vitae (CV) or Resume is your marketing tool. It is probably the first view a prospective employer will have of you.

Remember, first impressions count, so work hard on preparing your CV. Its function isn't to get you a job; it's to get you an interview. It is the interview that gets you the job.

When you're preparing your CV, be aware that you have about 30 seconds to impress the reader; and remember the reader is far more inclined to say no than yes. The quantity of CV's received for every vacancy is enormous. The person scanning CV's is looking for only one or two to progress to interview; all the rest are going to be rejected.

Your CV needs to be no more than 2 pages long; one page is often sufficient. It must be neat, concise and accurate. It should be printed on white 100gsm paper in 11pt Times New Roman script. Don't use coloured paper; and don't use covers or binders, they only get in the way.

A CV needs to tell the prospective employer three things:
- What does this applicant offer our business?
- What can he/she do for us?
- How do I contact him/her if required for an interview?

To answer those questions, a good CV needs to set out your experiences and your achievements. The prospective employer will then be able to tell if you meet the criteria they are looking for.

From the top down, your CV should include:
- Your Name
- Your Age
- A brief summary of your credentials for employment and the type of work you are looking for*
- A schedule of your qualifications, training and education with dates
- A chronological list, with dates, of your working history, starting with the most recent
  - o Include bullet points of your main responsibilities and achievements
  - o Include full time, part time, voluntary and charitable work
- A brief summary of your personal interests
- Your contact details

Remember your CV is a selling document. It needs to be neatly set out with no spelling mistakes. It needs to be concise with no waffle or padding. Include only what is relevant. Exclude anything that is negative. Keep it factual; avoid opinions and viewpoints.

**\*Examples of your credentials summary:**
- *A senior executive with considerable experience of managing manufacturing companies; seeking employment as a general manager or managing director*
- *15 years experience as a cabinet maker, seeking work in production or assembly environment*
- *School leaver with initiative and pleasant manner seeking work in a retail or hospitality environment*
- *Qualified child minder with 5 years experience seeking part time work in a crèche or nursery*
- *Recently qualified bricklayer seeking work in construction environment*
- *Hard working labourer seeking any kind of manual work*
- *Retired policeman seeking opportunity in security industry*
- *Experienced chamber maid seeking opportunity in hotel or catering sector*
- *Ex soldier seeking delivery driving or van sales job*
- *Recent graduate with mechanical engineering degree seeking position in motor industry*
- *15 years experienced rigid truck driver, clean C licence, seeking driving/delivery job*

An example of a fictitious CV is shown over.

CURRICULUM VITAE
# JACK MURPHY
Age 35
**Qualified gas fitter, Corgi registered, seeking employment
as a gas fitting supervisor**

## Qualifications & Education:
2005 DIT Dublin – Diploma in Gas Engineering
2004 Bord Gais – Testing Domestic Boilers and Heaters,
Certification Course
2004 Bord Gais - Working with Gas Safety Course
2003 FAS Dublin - Advanced Pipework Course
2001 FAS Dublin – Soldering, Pipe Bending and Thread Cutting
Course
1980 – 1990 Clontarf Community School – Leaving Certificate; 4
passes, 3 honours

## Employment History:
2003 to December 2008 – Breslaw Engineering, Gas Installers
- Team Leader responsible for 5 fitters
- Planning and supervising installation of replacement
  domestic boilers and follow up servicing
- 450 successful installations
- Resolving service queries to over 2,000 consumers in
  North Dublin
- Responsible for booking out materials and delivery to
  installation addresses
- Personally responsible for carrying out quality and safety
  checks, commissioning and sign off
1996 to 2003 – Dunboyne Plumbing and Heating Ltd – Heating
Engineers
- Fitter installing industrial boilers and heating systems
- Promoted to Gang Leader supervising 3 fitters
1990 to 1996 – Accrinton Manufacturing - Engineering Works
- Maintenance Engineer responsible for efficient
  running and operation of machine shop plant

- Carrying out planned maintenance routines and repairs as needed
- Purchasing and stock control of components, lubricants and consumables
- Providing 24 hour call out cover
- Awarded special service award for excellence and commitment to company objective scheme

## Personal Interests:

- Vintage Car Rallying
- Founder Member of NCD Vintage Car Association
- Assembling and flying model aircraft

## Contact Details:

Jack Murphy
24 Ardleigh Green Avenue, Clontarf, Dublin 6
Home Phone: 01 426445   Mobile: 086 654786
Email: jackymurphy102@hotmail.com

**Register your details with recruitment websites.** There are numerous recruitment web sites on the internet. Take a look at Loadzajobs.ie and fas.ie.

Googling recruitment will reveal other sites of interest.

There are also sites specialising in construction, nursing, sales jobs, executive vacancies and so on.

All web-sites have an easy to follow registration process which includes capturing your personal, employment and education details.

**Register with local and specialised recruitment agencies.** Check the Golden Pages or Google the internet for local recruitment agencies and agencies that specialise in your particular sector. Send them your CV with a covering letter asking that you be considered for any vacancies they may have on their books. Tell them you are available to start work immediately.

**Regularly browse the recruitment websites like Loadzajobs.ie.** Make a point of browsing on a daily basis, the vacancies posted on recruitment websites you've registered with. Apply for all vacancies you believe you are suitably qualified for.

**Regularly visit your local FAS office to review vacancies.** FAS, the National Training and Employment Agency, have offices in most major towns. Call in at least once a week and check out the vacancies they have listed.

**Regularly review the local newspapers for vacancies.**
Local papers are a good source of vacancies. Make sure
to review them each week. They are usually available
free to read in your local library.

**Regularly review the national newspapers for
vacancies.** The Irish Independent and Irish Times
include a recruitment section on Thursday and Sunday.
The Evening Herald has a Classified Vacancies section
every day.

**Give your CV to local businesses.** Post, or if possible
deliver your CV to local businesses. If you are delivering
them yourself, ask if you can see the manager, introduce
yourself and explain that you are looking for work. Be
polite and friendly, and make sure you are appropriately
dressed.

**Send out speculative CV's.** A good approach may be to
identify companies that you would like to work for, or
that you believe would be interested in the type of
experience and skills that you possess. Write to them,
enclosing your CV and asking if you could be
considered for any vacancies that they may have.

**Keep a Job Hunters journal.** It is important that you
keep a record of all your job hunting activities. Make a
note of all applications, of where you send CV's, and
what responses you get.

You could also find out if there is a **Resource Centre for the Unemployed** or **Job Centre** near you. They operate in some counties and offer practical help in preparing CV's, getting ready for interviews and so on. They can also provide computer facilities and access to the internet. So check your local phonebook.

And don't forget to join the Job Seekers Union – they are setting up a network of job clubs across the country to help jobseekers help themselves create work. You can find them at www.thejobseekersunion.com

**A few words about interviews:**

- Do some research beforehand to find out as much about your potential employer as you can. It pays to look enthusiastic and well prepared.
- Make sure you know where the location for the interview is
- Give yourself plenty of time to get there
- Arrive a few minutes early
- Wear appropriate clothes
- Bring qualifications and references with you
- Don't be put off by the formality of the interview room or the fact that there might be more than one person interviewing you
- Be friendly but polite
- Pay particular attention to the questions you are asked
- Think about your answers before you give them
- Avoid controversial opinions or comments

When you are looking for a job in today's climate, it really is important to stay optimistic. Don't give up, even if you don't seem to be getting anywhere. It's not a reflection of you if all you seem to be getting is refusals; it's simply the lack of vacancies and the volume of applicants chasing the few that are out there. Keep trying, never give up; the job you are looking for might be just around the corner.

*'Success is nine tenths perspiration.'*

**Oh no, I've lost my job; what am I going to do now?**

I had no shoes and I grumbled,

Then I saw a man who had no feet.

**Oh no, I've lost my job; what am I going to do now?**

# SURVIVING LONG TERM UNEMPLOYMENT

If the recession continues for any length of time, it is possible that you might find yourself unemployed for several months or even longer.

If that is the case, it is going to be difficult for you. Assuming you have managed to get your finances under control, the biggest problems are going to be boredom, the possible loss of self esteem and the risk of depression.

How well you survive long term unemployment depends almost entirely on your state of mind. As I said in an earlier chapter; it isn't what happens in life that matters, it is your reaction to it.

If you ever studied science, you might have heard of something known as cause and effect. In simple terms, this means one thing leads to another; or put more scientifically, for every action there is a re-action.

You've lost your job; you can't do anything about that. A year later, you're still unemployed despite trying hard to get another job; you can't do much about that either, except keep looking for work.

So what are you left with? Your reaction to what's happening; that's what you're left with, and that you can do something about.

Your reaction to what's happening is completely within your control. I'm not preaching or trying to be smart; but when it comes down to it, it really is all about choices.

Let's look at two people, Jim and Seamus. They both worked for the same employer for 15 years and they both lost their job on the same day. Neither has been able to find work since.

Jim stays up late in the night staring at the TV. He's taken to drinking a bit too much. He lies in bed 'till lunchtime, then he mopes about the house all afternoon watching DVDs that he's seen a dozen times before. He doesn't read the newspapers. He doesn't go out. He's not eating very well, and he's smoking far too heavily. He's finding it hard to make ends meet. That's because he spends over half his dole money on booze and fags; although he'd never admit to that. He's fed up; he's depressed. He can't see the point in life anymore. He argues with his wife a lot. He's worried his marriage is on the rocks, but he doesn't make any attempt to improve his relationship with his wife.

Seamus gets up early, has breakfast and takes his new dog for a walk. He always wanted a dog when he was working, but he didn't really have the time for one. He wouldn't be without his dog now. If the weather's good he does a bit of gardening. He started a vegetable

garden; something he always wanted to do, but didn't
have the time when he was working. He alternates the
cooking with his wife. He enjoys experimenting with
new recipes and has become a bit of gourmet chef; at
least that what he likes to think. After lunch, he goes to
the adult learning centre. He's started to become quite
adept on the computer and the internet; something he
knew nothing about when he was working. He has a
computer at home now; he's planning to set up a little
business trading used furniture on eBay. Once a week he
talks to his brother in Australia and his sister in Canada
via email; he'd lost touch with both of them when he
working. He's joined a bridge club with his wife;
something he always wanted to do but never had the
time. On Thursdays he helps out at the local SVP centre.
He's become a friend of the local hospital and visits
patients who would otherwise have no visitors. He
doesn't get paid, but it makes him feel good to think he
might be helping people worse off than himself. He's
joined a walking club; nothing too strenuous, but the
exercise is good and it's much cheaper than the golf
club. He goes out with his wife on Saturday night;
nothing too spectacular, the cinema, the local theatre, a
couple of drinks in the local pub. On Sunday he sings in
the church choir; something he always wanted to do but
never found the time when he was working. His wife
prepares a Sunday roast; Seamus helps prepare the
vegetables and does the dishes. He reads a good quality
Sunday paper from cover to cover. He likes to keep up to
date with the news. He's adjusted well to his lower level
of income. He puts a bit aside each week for a camping
holiday in Donegal that he always promised himself

when he was working, but never managed to get around
to.

*"What's the difference between Jim and Seamus?"*
"Seamus has a much better life."
*"Why?"*
"Because Seamus makes the effort."
*"Are you saying Jim is lazy?"*
"I'm saying he doesn't try."
*"But it's easy for Seamus; he's got the right attitude."*
"Precisely!"

> *'The power of positive thinking.'* Norman
> Vincent Peale

I know; it's easy to be glib. Losing your job is rough. It's
a dreadful thing to happen to someone. Nobody would
deny that. It can come with a lot of baggage too:

- Boredom – *What am I going to do 'till bedtime?*
- Feelings of failure – *What good am I if I can't earn a decent wage?*
- Low self esteem – *I'm worthless now I've got no job.*
- Feelings of despair– *Who'd want me, I've been out of work so long?*
- Feelings of hopelessness – *It's useless, I'll never get another job.*
- Shame – *I don't want to face anybody.*
- Self pity – *Poor me!*

- Self loathing – *I hate what I've become.*
- Envy of those at work – *It's alright for them, they're working.*

The big risk, if these negative feelings are allowed to fester, is depression.

Everybody feels a bit down in the dumps now and again. It's normal for set-backs to upset us, for the weather to get us down, for boredom to make us lazy, or our temper to get the better of us sometimes. Depression is where these negative feelings are long lasting and debilitating.

The symptoms of depression include:
- Loss of interest in life
- Cutting yourself off from family and friends
- Difficulty sleeping
- Loss of appetite or excessive appetite
- Crying
- Paying less attention to yourself
- Suicidal thoughts

Depression is a medical condition. It is not as simple as 'just pull yourself together'. It needs to be treated by a professional (doctor, psychiatrist or counsellor).

If you feel you are depressed seek help; modern medicines and therapies are very effective in treating depression.

Let's hope depression doesn't come knocking on your door. If it does, go to your doctor; he will be able to help you. (Also see the chapter on Seeking Help).

*A positive attitude will go a long way to making your experience with long term unemployment a positive one.*

Here are some ideas to make life more interesting and help you prosper:

- Join your local Job Seekers Union
- Gardening
- Join a walking club
- Become computer literate
- Join a bridge club
- Join a social networking site like Facebook
- Knit a scarf or a jumper
- Keep chickens
- Enrol on a FAS course
- Join the library
- Get a bicycle
- Start a vegetable plot
- Look for old friends on Friends Reunited
- Join the Garda Reserve
- Get sponsored to walk, run, talk, or have your head shaved for charity
- Learn to swim
- Build a model airplane
- Join the Toast Masters
- Enrol in an Adult Education class
- Take up tennis or golf
- Buy a dog or other pet
- Parachute jump for charity
- Plan a cheap holiday
- Join an on-line dating site
- Start a craft hobby
- Join the Army Cadets
- Take up fishing
- Learn to be a mechanic

- Take up Yoga or meditation
- Start a collection of something unusual
- Decorate your bedroom
- Join your local Tidy Towns group
- Take up art classes
- Start a herb garden
- Take up dancing lessons
- Cultivate a window box
- Join a local sports club
- Read books
- Visit a Farmer's Market
- Get a budgerigar
- See if your local hospital needs any voluntary helpers
- Paint the house
- Set up an eBay trading business
- Listen to music
- Volunteer to help St Vincent de Paul
- Take up cooking, experiment with new recipes
- Go to a lunch-time concert at the National Concert Hall
- Take up busking
- Do a crossword or Sudoku puzzle
- Join the St John's Ambulance or the Red Cross
- Learn calligraphy
- Cultivate indoor plants
- Visit museums or art galleries
- Ask your TD to organise a visit to the Dail for you
- Join a voluntary organisation
- Start and complete a jigsaw puzzle
- Bake your own bread, cakes, biscuits, pastries
- Become an active member of your local church
- Make home-made jam
- If there is a prison near you, see if they need any voluntary helpers
- Join the Civil defence

OK so we've established there really are lots of things you can do if you put your mind to it. At this point there are two words I want you to think about, inertia and momentum.

- Inertia is the physical force that keeps stationary things from moving
- Momentum is the physical force that keeps things going once they've started to move

If you've ever tried to bump start a car, you'll have experienced the forces of inertia and momentum. Can you remember how hard it was to get the car to move when you first started to push it? That was the effect of inertia. You can probably also remember how much easier it was to keep it going once it had started moving; that was the effect of momentum.

It's inertia that keeps you flopped in the armchair staring at the TV, rather than getting up and doing something. It's inertia that's making you fed up and bored. It's inertia that's going to lead to depression.

It's amazing how much better you'll feel, if you can overcome that inertia, get out of the chair and start doing things. That's the effect of momentum. It's momentum that makes you feel energised and optimistic.

The best way to survive long term unemployment is to overcome inertia and create a momentum for yourself. It's amazing the difference it will make.

There's something else to bear in mind when you're sitting on the couch staring at the TV; it's called the domino effect. It means, once you start doing things, other things will start to happen. Put another way around it also means, nothing will happen for you unless and until you start doing something.

*If nothing changes; nothing changes!*

Doing nothing is the worst possible thing. Don't let yourself get stuck in a rut; get off your arse and do something. If you don't, you'll be stuck on your arse forever.

*'Every day do something that will inch you towards a better tomorrow.'*

A few other pearls of wisdom that you might find helpful:

- Check out Ryanair for cheap (sometimes free) flights. You'll be amazed where you can go if you're flexible
- Buses can be a cheap way of seeing Ireland
- The radio is a good alternative to TV
- Music is the food of the soul; listen to your favourite tunes and sing or dance along
- Laughter is the best medicine; watch the comedy re-runs of Father Ted, Del Boy, Porridge and so on, and laugh out loud

Finally, have you ever considered a change of career? Have you ever thought about starting your own small business? What about learning a new skill or a new trade?

All things are possible. Check out FAS, your local County or City Enterprise Board and your local VEC to see what possibilities are available.

Let me wish you good luck in your brush with unemployment and offer you some inspirational thoughts:

- *One way to get the most out of life is to look upon it as an adventure*
- *No great man ever complains of a lack of opportunities*
- *A wise man will make more opportunities than he finds*

Finally, I can think of no better way to end this little book than to leave you with the words of former US President John F Kennedy...

**"The Chinese word for crisis is composed of two characters.
One represents danger, and the other represents opportunity."**

\*\*\*

## Fortune favours the bold

# Useful Contact Addresses:

The organisations listed below are there to help. Never be shy about asking them for assistance – that's what they're there for.

**Local Health Centre** – for Supplementary Welfare Allowance, Mortgage Interest Supplement, Rental Supplement or Medical Card applications.
**See any phone book** for details

**Local Social Welfare Office** - to register for Unemployment and Other Benefits.
**See any phone book** for details

**Citizens Information Service** – for information on social and civil rights, housing, employment, health, legal aid and so on.
**LoCall 1890 777 121** for your nearest office

**FAS Training and Employment Authority** – for help finding a job or a training course. **Freephone 1800 611 116** for your nearest office

**NERA National Employment Rights Authority** - for general enquiries on employment rights, redundancy entitlements, notice period, holiday pay etc. **LoCall 1890 80 80 90**

**Employment Appeals Tribunal**- for specific enquiries about redundancy entitlements, unfair dismissal, minimum wage etc. **LoCall 1890 220 222**

**Social Welfare Appeals Office** – for queries relating to your unemployment or other welfare entitlements. **LoCall 1890 747 434**

**Department of Social and Family Affairs, Scope Section** – to determine whether you are employed or self employed. **Telephone: 01 - 673 2585**

**Resource Centre for the Unemployed** or **Job Centre** – provide practical help in finding another job. See your **local phonebook** for details

**HSE Helpline** – for supplementary welfare, emergency financial help and medical card enquiries. **Callsave 1850 24 1850**

**MABS Money Advice & Budgeting Service** – free and confidential help for people in debt. **LoCall 1890 83438**

**St Vincent de Paul** – for anybody who needs any kind of help.
**See any phone book** for details

**AWARE** – for help if you are depressed. **LoCall 1890 30 30 30 2**

**Samaritans** – someone to talk to if you're depressed or suicidal.
**Callsave 1850 60 90 90**

**The Job Seekers Union** –
**www.thejobseekersunion.com**